Handy Michigan Genealogy Handbook

I0439895

Gary L. Morris

©2015 Gary L. Morris

ISBN-13: 978-1508405627

ISBN-10: 150840562X

Table of Contents

Notes

Genealogical Research in Michigan

Tracing your family history in Michigan can be a fascinating trip through time. As one of the earliest areas in America settled by Europeans, there are a wealth of genealogical records and resources for tracing your family history in Michigan. Tracking these records down can be an ominous task, but don't worry, we know just where they are, and we'll show you which records you'll need, and help you to understand:

- What they are
- Where to find them
- How to use them

These records can be found both online and off, so we'll introduce you to online websites, indexes and databases, as well as brick-and-mortar repositories and other institutions that will help with your research in Michigan. So that you will have a more comprehensive understanding of these records, we have provided a brief history of the "The Wolverine State" to illustrate what type of records may have been generated during specific time periods. That information will assist you in pinpointing times and locations on which to focus the search for your Michigan ancestors and their records.

A Brief History of Michigan

It is believed that Native Americans first settled Michigan as early as 11,000 B.C. The first European explorer to venture into the area was the French explorer Étienne Brûlé in the early 17th century. The area was claimed by France and was part of French Louisiana from 1682 to 1762. During this period the fist settlement was established in 1701 at Fort Pontchartrain du Detroit, now known as the city of Detroit.

After France's defeat in the French and Indian Wars, the area was ceded to Great Britain. Great Britain subsequently ceded the region to America after it was defeated in the Revolutionary War. Michigan became part of the Northwest Territory in 1787, and remained so until 1800. Michigan became a separate territory in 1806, and when the Erie Canal opened in 1825 connecting the Great lakes with the Hudson River, large numbers of settlers flocked to the area. A state Constitution was approved in 1835, but Michigan's admittance to the Union was delayed by a border dispute with Ohio known as the Toledo War.

Michigan finally became a state on January 26, 1337, and when iron and copper deposits were discovered, the construction of the Soo Locks began and was completed in 1855. In addition to mining, logging and agriculture became important industries, and Michigan's economy began to grow. The growing economy and population allowed Michigan to make a substantial contribution to the Union cause during the American Civil War. Ninety thousand troops from Michigan, including General George Custer fought on the Union side, and played major roles in several major battles, especially at Gettysburg.

Important Dates in Michigan History

1701– First permanent settlement established at Fort Pontchartrain du Detroit
1763 – Ceded from France to Great Britain
1774 – Part of Quebec
1783 – Ceded from Great Britain to United States
1787 – Part of Northwest Territory
1800 – Part of Indiana Territory
1805 – Created as separate territory
1812 – Detroit captured by British during War of 1812
1835 – State constitution written
1837 - Statehood

Famous Battles Fought in Michigan

There is only one battle of note that has ever been fought on Michigan soil, but it was a deadly and bloody conflict. The **Battle of Frenchtown**, also known as the River Raisin Massacre or Battle of the River Raisin, was a series of conflicts that took place from January 18–23, 1813 during the War of 1812.

These battle accounts that do exist can be very effective in uncovering the military records of your ancestor. They can tell you what regiments fought in which battles, and often include the names and ranks of many officers and enlisted men.

Battle of Frenchtown:
http://www.riverraisinbattlefield.org/the_battles.htm

Common Michigan Genealogical Issues and Resources to Overcome Them

Boundary Changes: Boundary changes are a common obstacle when researching Michigan ancestors. You could be searching for an ancestor's record in one county when in fact it is stored in a different one due to historical county boundary changes.

The **Atlas of Historical County Boundaries** can help you to overcome that problem. It provides a chronological listing of every boundary change that has occurred in the history of Michigan.

Atlas of Historical County Boundaries link to: http://publications.newberry.org/ahcbp/documents/MI_Consolidated _Chronology.htm#Consolidated_Chronology

Name Changes: Surname changes, variations, and misspellings can complicate genealogical research. It is important to check all spelling variations. Soundex, a program that indexes names by sound, is a useful first step, but you can't rely on it completely as some name variations result in different Soundex codes. The surnames could be different, but the first name may be different too. You can also find records filed under initials, middle names, and nicknames as well, so you will need to **get creative with surname variations** and spellings in order to cover all the possibilities. For help with surname variations read our instructional article on **How to Use Soundex**.

get creative with surname variations: http://obituarieshelp.org/blog/?p=634

How to Use Soundex: http://obituarieshelp.org/blog/?p=505

Michigan Genealogical Organizations and Archives

Genealogical resources include not only records, but the organizations that house them, or can direct you to them. These institutions include: *Archives, Libraries, Genealogical Societies, Family History Centers, Universities, Churches, and Museums.*

Following are links to their websites, their physical addresses, and a summary of the records you can find there.

<u>Archives and Libraries</u>

Library of Michigan - African American records, business records, census records, land records, manuscripts, military records, mining records, Native American records, probate records, railroad records, women's records, Vital records 1867-1994, state census records 1827- 1894, Civil War service records, cemetery records, historical newspapers, Indexes to naturalizations for more than 30 Michigan counties, Michigan County Clerks directory, and many other genealogical guides and resources

702 W. Kalamazoo St.
Lansing, MI 48909-7507
Tel: 517-373-1300
Fax: (517) 373-3381
Email: librarian@michigan.gov

Mailing Address:

702 W. Kalamazoo St.
7507P.O. Box 30007
Lansing, MI 48909-7507P.O. Box 30007

Library of Michigan:
http://www.michigan.gov/libraryofmichigan/0,2351,7-160-18635---,00.html

Western Michigan University – manuscript collection, county records, state records, census records, oral histories, books, periodicals, and historical newspapers

Kalamazoo
MI 49008-5200
Tel: (269) 387-1000

Western Michigan University:
http://www.wmich.edu/library/collections/archives/collections

National Archives Great Lake Region (Chicago) – court records, naturalization records, Chinese exclusions, Native American records and more

7358 South Pulaski Road
Chicago, IL 60629
Telephone: 312-581-7816

National Archives Great Lake Region (Chicago):
http://www.archives.gov/chicago/

Michigan Genealogical and Historical Societies

Genealogical and historical societies have access to extensive catalogues of genealogical data. They are also able to offer expert guidance for genealogical researchers. Many members are professional genealogists who are most willing to share their expertise in finding ancestors.

Michigan Genealogy Council – miscellaneous genealogical resources

P.O. Box 80953
Lansing, MI 48908-0953
Email: migencouncil@att.net

Michigan Genealogy Council: http://mimgc.org/

Detroit Society for Genealogical Research – cemetery records, surname registry, periodicals, genealogy forums and more

Detroit Public Library
c/o Burton Historical Collection
5201 Woodward Ave.
Detroit, MI 48202-4007
Email: webmaster@dsgr.org

Detroit Society for Genealogical Research: http://www.dsgr.org/

Western Michigan Genealogical Society – historical newspapers, school census reports, veterans records, manuscripts, family histories, county records, county histories, and statewide census records
c/o Grand Rapids
Public Library
111 Library Street NE
Grand Rapids, MI 49503-3268
Email: wmgs@wmgs.org

Western Michigan Genealogical Society: http://data.wmgs.org/

French-Canadian Heritage Society of Michigan – family histories, marriage records, records of the French National Archives, pioneers list, county and community histories, and more

Mount Clemens Public Library
150 Cass Ave.
Mount Clemens, MI 48043-2297
(586) 469-6200
(586) 469-6668, fax

Mailing Address:

Post Office Box 1900
Royal Oak MI 48068-1900

French-Canadian Heritage Society of Michigan: http://fchsm.org/

Historical Society of Michigan – miscellaneous genealogical resources

5815 Executive Drive
Lansing MI 48911
Phone: (517) 324-1828
Fax: (517) 324-4370
Email: hsm@hsmichigan.org

Historical Society of Michigan: http://www.hsmichigan.org/

Irish Genealogical Society of Michigan – resources for researching Irish ancestors in Michigan

c/o Gaelic League/Irish American Club
2068 Michigan Avenue
Detroit MI 48216-1303

Irish Genealogical Society of Michigan: http://miigsm.org/

Jewish Genealogical Society of Michigan – miscellaneous resources for researching Jewish ancestors in Michigan including a vast library containing books, periodicals, videotapes, audiotapes, microfiche, and CD-ROMs, and especially a huge collection of periodicals

Holocaust Memorial Center
2nd Floor
28123 Orchard Lake Road
Farmington Hills, MI 48334-3738
Tel: (248) 553-2400 ext. 16

Jewish Genealogical Society of Michigan: http://jgsmi.org/

Additional Michigan Genealogical Resources

Michigan Mailing Lists

Mailing lists are internet based facilities that use email to distribute a single message to all who subscribe to it. When information on a particular surname, new records, or any other important genealogy information related to the mailing list topic becomes available, the subscribers are alerted to it. Joining a mailing list is an excellent way to stay up to date on Michigan genealogy research topics. Rootsweb have an extensive listing of **Michigan Mailing Lists** on a variety of topics.

Michigan Mailing Lists:
http://lists.rootsweb.ancestry.com/index/usa/MI/misc.html

Michigan Message Boards

A message board is another internet based facility where people can post questions about a specific genealogy topic and have it answered by other genealogists. If you have questions about a surname, record type, or research topic, you can post your question and other researchers and genealogists will help you with the answer. Be sure to check back regularly, as the answers are not emailed to you. The Michigan message boards at **Rootsweb** are completely free to use.

Rootsweb:
http://boards.rootsweb.com/localities.northam.usa.states/mb.ashx

Michigan Newspapers and Periodicals

Many genealogy periodicals and historical newspapers contain reprinted copies of family genealogies, transcripts of family Bible records, information about local records and archives, census indexes, church records, queries, land records, obituaries, court records, cemetery records, and wills. The following sites have historical Michigan newspapers and periodicals that you can search online or on-site.

Library of Michigan – collection includes titles from all 83 counties, and includes a special index of newspapers that are especially useful to family historians

702 W. Kalamazoo St.
Lansing, MI 48909-7507
Tel: 517-373-1300
Fax: (517) 373-3381
Email: librarian@michigan.gov

Mailing Address:

702 W. Kalamazoo St.
7507P.O. Box 30007
Lansing, MI 48909-7507P.O. Box 30007

Library of Michigan:
http://www.michigan.gov/libraryofmichigan/0,2351,7-160-50206_18643---,00.html

Western Michigan University – Newspapers for several towns in southwestern Michigan and part of the Michigan Newspaper Project

Kalamazoo
MI 49008-5200
Tel: (269) 387-1000

Western Michigan University:
http://www.wmich.edu/library/collections/archives/collections

Western Michigan Genealogical Society – West Michigan Newspapers - index to Death Notices and Obituaries published in the Grand Rapids Press and Grand Rapids Herald from 1910 to present, Grand Rapids EWA from 1956 and 1957

c/o Grand Rapids
Public Library
111 Library Street NE
Grand Rapids, MI 49503-3268
Email: wmgs@wmgs.org

Western Michigan Genealogical Society: http://data.wmgs.org/

GenealogyBank.com – free searchable database of Michigan newspaper archives, 1837–1995

GenealogyBank.com:
http://www.genealogybank.com/gbnk/newspapers/explore/USA/Michigan/

Library of Congress Digital Newspaper Directory – free searchable database of historical U.S. newspapers dating from 1690-present

Library of Congress Digital Newspaper Directory:
http://chroniclingamerica.loc.gov/search/titles/

The Online Books Page – links to historical Michigan books and periodicals available for viewing online, dating from mid-16th century

The Online Books Page: http://onlinebooks.library.upenn.edu/

NewspaperArchive.com – largest online database of historical newspapers in the world.

NewspaperArchive.com: http://newspaperarchive.com/

Historical Michigan Maps and Gazetteers

Maps are an integral part of genealogical research. They help us to locate landmarks, towns, cities, parishes, states, provinces, waterways and roads and streets. They also help us to determine when and where boundary changes might have taken place, and give us a visualization of the area we're researching in.

For locating place names, a gazetteer is the best possible resource for any genealogist. Gazetteers are also sometimes called "place name dictionaries", and can help you to locate the area in which you need to conduct research. Below are links to the maps and gazetteers for research in Michigan.

Peabody GNIS Service – Michigan:
http://peabody.research.yale.edu/cgi-bin/Query.GNIS?ST=Michigan&SU=1

Color Landform Atlas – Michigan:
http://fermi.jhuapl.edu/states/mi_0.html

1985 U.S. Atlas: http://www.livgenmi.com/1895/MI/

Michigan Hometown Locator:
http://michigan.hometownlocator.com/

Michigan City Directories
.

City directories are similar to telephone directories in that they list the residents of a particular area. The difference though is what is important to genealogists, and that is they pre-date telephone directories. You can find an ancestor's information such as their street address, place of employment, occupation, or the name of their spouse. A one-stop-shop for finding city directories in Michigan is the **Michigan Online Historical Directories** which contains a listing of every available online historical directory related to Michigan.

Michigan Online Historical Directories:
https://sites.google.com/site/onlinedirectorysite/Home/usa/mi

Bentley Historical Library – University of Michigan - large collection of city and county directories

1150 Beal Avenue
Ann Arbor, MI 48109-2113 U.S.A
Tel: 734.764.3482
Fax: 734.936.1333
Email: bentley.ref@umich.edu

Bentley Historical Library:
http://bentley.umich.edu/research/guides/directories.php

Michigan Genealogical Records

<u>Birth, Death, Marriage and Divorce Records</u> – Also known as vital records, birth, death, and marriage certificates are the most basic, yet most important records attached to your ancestor. The reason for their importance is that they not only place your ancestor in a specific place at a definite time, but potentially connect the individual to other relatives. Below is a list of repositories and websites where you can find Michigan vital records.

Michigan Department of Community Health - records of births, deaths, and marriages that occurred in Michigan and were filed with the state as early as 1867, and divorce records as early as 1897.

201 Townsend Street
Capitol View Bldg, 3rd Floor
Lansing MI 48933
Tel: 517-373-3740

Michigan Department of Community Health link:
http://www.michigan.gov/mdch/0,4612,7-132-4645---,00.html

Library of Michigan – Births, 1867-1915, Marriages 1867-1921, 1950-1969, 1867-1925; Divorces 1897-1969, 1897-1922; Deaths 1867-1914, 1867-1897, 1897-1920

702 W. Kalamazoo St.
Lansing, MI 48909-7507
Tel: 517-373-1300
Fax: (517) 373-3381
Email: librarian@michigan.gov

Mailing Address:
702 W. Kalamazoo St.
7507P.O. Box 30007
Lansing, MI 48909-7507P.O. Box 30007

Library of Michigan:
http://www.michigan.gov/libraryofmichigan/0,2351,7-160-18635---,00.html

Western Michigan Genealogical Society – Kent County Deaths Index, Kent County Marriages 1845 – 1929

c/o Grand Rapids
Public Library
111 Library Street NE
Grand Rapids, MI 49503-3268
Email: wmgs@wmgs.org

Western Michigan Genealogical Society: http://data.wmgs.org/

Family Search has the following indexes which can be searched online for free:

Michigan Births and Christenings, 1775-1995:
https://familysearch.org/search/collection/1675348

Michigan Births, 1867-1902:
https://familysearch.org/search/collection/1459684

Michigan County Marriages, 1820-1935 link to:
https://familysearch.org/search/collection/1810350

Michigan Death Certificates, 1921-1952:
https://familysearch.org/search/collection/1968532

Michigan Death Index, 1971-1996:
https://familysearch.org/search/collection/1949333

Michigan Deaths and Burials, 1800-1995:
https://familysearch.org/search/collection/1675357

Michigan Deaths, 1867-1897:
https://familysearch.org/search/collection/1916040

Michigan Marriages, 1822-1995:
https://familysearch.org/search/collection/1675359

Michigan Marriages, 1868-1925:
https://familysearch.org/search/collection/1452395

Census Reports

Census records are among the most important genealogical documents for placing your ancestor in a particular place at a specific time. Like BDM records, they can also lead you to other ancestors, particularly those who were living under the authority of the head of household.

Federal census records for Michigan exist from 1790–1930 and can be found at:

Western Michigan University – Michigan census available on microfilm through 1930
Kalamazoo
MI 49008-5200
Tel: (269) 387-1000

Western Michigan University:
http://www.wmich.edu/library/collections/archives/collections

National Archives – Federal census Schedules for all states, 1790-1940
8601 Adelphi Road
College Park, MD 20740-6001
Tel: 1-866-272-6272

National Archives: http://www.archives.gov/research/census/

Library of Michigan – variety of county schedules and enumerations
702 W. Kalamazoo St.
Lansing, MI 48909-7507
Tel: 517-373-1300
Fax: (517) 373-3381
Email: librarian@michigan.gov

Library of Michigan:
http://www.michigan.gov/documents/mhc_sa_circular09_49695_7.pdf

The **Free Census Project** has transcribed many Michigan indexes and new material is added daily

Free Census Project: http://usgwcensus.org/cenfiles/mi.htm

Access Genealogy – Michigan county census records from 1820-1930

Access Genealogy: http://www.accessgenealogy.com/census/michigan-1820-1930-census-records.htm

African American Census Schedules Online – slave schedules, mortality schedules, slave-owners census

African American Census Schedules Online: http://www.afrigeneas.com/aacensus/

Native Americans in Census Records (US National Archives): http://www.archives.gov/research/census/native-americans/

Michigan Church Records

Church and synagogue records are a valuable resource, especially for baptisms, marriages, and burials that took place before 1900. You will need to at least have an idea of your ancestor's religious denomination, and in most cases you will have to visit a brick and mortar establishment to view them.

Most church records are kept by the individual church, although in some denominations, records are placed in a regional archive or maintained at the diocesan level. Local Historical Societies are sometimes the repository for the state's older church records. Below are links archives that maintain church records, as well as a few databases that can be viewed online.

The **Family History Library** contains many church records from a variety of denominations on microfilm.

Family History Library:
http://familysearch.org/learn/wiki/en/Family_History_Library

Bentley Historical Library – University of Michigan – many denominational records from around the state, also funeral directory records

1150 Beal Avenue
Ann Arbor, MI 48109-2113 U.S.A
Tel: 734.764.3482
Fax: 734.936.1333
Email: bentley.ref@umich.edu

Bentley Historical Library:
http://bentley.umich.edu/research/genealogy/dates.php#church

Central Repositories for Denominational Records

Baptist

Kalamazoo College
Upjohn Library
1200 Academy Street
Kalamazoo, MI 49006
Lisa Murphy, Archivist
Email: lisa.murphy@kzoo.edu
Phone: 269-337-7151

Upjohn Library: http://www.kzoo.edu/is/library/index.html

Church of Jesus Christ of Latter-day Saints (Mormons)

Early Mormon Church records for Michigan can be found on film located at the LDS Family History Library in Salt Lake City and can be searched via the **Family History Library Catalog**

Family History Library Catalog:
https://familysearch.org/eng/Library/FHLC/frameset_fhlc.asp

Lutheran

Evangelical Lutheran Church in America (ELCA Archives)
8765 West Higgins Road
Chicago, IL 60631-4198
Phone: (312) 380-2818
Fax: (312)-380-2977
E-mail Address: archives@elca.org

Evangelical Lutheran Church in America (ELCA Archives):
http://www.elca.org/

Methodist

Shipman Library Adrian College
110 South Madison Street
Adrian, MI 49221
Phone: (517) 265-5161
Fax: (517) 264-3331

Shipman Library Adrian College: http://adrian.edu/library/

Roman Catholic

Archdiocese of Detroit
1234 Washington Boulevard
Detroit, MI 48226
Phone: (313) 237-5800
Fax: (313) 237-4642

Archdiocese of Detroit: http://www.aod.org/

Diocese of Gaylord
611 W. North Street
Gaylord, MI 49735
Phone: (989) 732-5147

Diocese of Gaylord:
http://www.dioceseofgaylord.org/inside/archives-44/

Diocese of Kalamazoo
215 N. Westnedge Ave.
Kalamazoo, MI 49007
Phone: (269) 349-8714

Diocese of Kalamazoo: http://www.dioceseofkalamazoo.org/

Diocese of Lansing
300 West Ottawa
Lansing, MI 48933
Phone: (517) 342-2440
Fax: (517) 343-2515

Diocese of Lansing: http://www.dioceseoflansing.org/archives

Diocese of Marquette
444 South Fourth Street
P.O. Box 550
Marquette, MI 49855
Phone: (906) 225-1141
Fax: (906) 225-0437

Diocese of Marquette: http://www.dioceseofmarquette.org/

Diocese of Saginaw
5800 Weiss Street
Saginaw, MI 48603-2799
Phone: (517) 799-7910
Fax: (517) 797-6670

Diocese of Saginaw: http://www.saginaw.org/

Michigan Military Records

More than 40 million Americans have participated in some time of war service since America was colonized. The chance of finding your ancestor amongst those records is exceptionally high. Military records can even reveal individuals who never actually served, such as those who registered for the two World Wars but were never called to duty.

Below are a number of links to websites and archives that contain Michigan military records.

Archives of Michigan – Michigan Volunteer Descriptive Rolls, 1838-1919, Rosters of the Michigan Veterans Facility, (veterans, 1885-1982; women dependents, 1894-1980), Muster rolls of Grand Army of the Republic (GAR) Posts, Civil War Grave Registrations, Federal Military Service Records, U.S. Pension Application Files and U.S. Bounty-Land Warrant Application Files (officers who served before June 30, 1916, enlisted men who served before 1896), and Confederate armed forces (1861-1865), Black Hawk War (1832), Toledo War (1835), and Patriot War (1838–39) records

Michigan Historical Center
702 West Kalamazoo St.
Lansing Michigan 48913
Tel: 517-373-3559
E-Mail: archives@michigan.gov

Archives of Michigan: http://www.michigan.gov/dnr/0,4570,7-153-54463_19313-98931--,00.html

U.S. National Archives – WWI Draft registration cards, casualties lists, WWI and WWII service records, Korean War records, Vietnam War records, Civil War and Spanish-American War records, and casualties lists.

U.S. National Archives:
http://www.archives.gov/research/military/veterans/online.html

US Department of Veterans Affairs Nationwide Gravesite Locator – includes information on veterans and their family members buried in veterans and military cemeteries having a government grave marker.

US Department of Veterans Affairs Nationwide Gravesite Locator: http://gravelocator.cem.va.gov/

You may also find your ancestor's military records in the following databases:

United States General Index to Pension Files, 1861-1934: https://familysearch.org/search/collection/1919699

United States Index to Service Records, War with Spain, 1898: https://familysearch.org/search/collection/1919583

United States Index to Indian Wars Pension Files, 1892-1926 – military pension records of soldiers who fought in the Indian Wars between 1817 and 1898

United States Index to Indian Wars Pension Files, 1892-1926: https://familysearch.org/search/collection/1979427

United States Registers of Enlistments in the U.S. Army, 1798-1914 - index of men who enlisted in the United States Army, 1798-1914.

United States Registers of Enlistments in the U.S. Army, 1798-1914: https://familysearch.org/search/collection/1880762

United States Mexican War Pension Index, 1887-1926: https://familysearch.org/search/collection/1979390

Civil War Soldiers Service Records - Service records for both Union and Confederate soldiers indexed by soldier's name, rank, and unit.

Civil War Soldier Service Records: http://go.fold3.com/civilwar_records/

<u>Michigan Cemetery Records</u>

As convenient as it is to search cemetery records online, keep in mind that there are a few disadvantages over visiting a cemetery in person. They are:

- Tombstone information is not always accurately transcribed
- The arrangement of the graves in a cemetery can be crucial as family members are often buried next to each other or in the same grave. This arrangement is not always preserved in the alphabetical indexes that are found online.

With that information in mind, the following websites have databases that can be searched online for Michigan Cemetery records.

Michigan Tombstone Transcription Project - death and burial records

Michigan Tombstone Transcription Project:
http://www.usgwtombstones.org/michigan/mitstable.htm

African American Cemeteries Online – African American, slave, and Native American cemetery records

African American Cemeteries Online:
http://africanamericancemeteries.com

Access Genealogy – huge database of Michigan cemetery record transcriptions

Access Genealogy:
http://www.accessgenealogy.com/cemetery/michigan-cemetery-records.htm

Find a Grave – over 100 million grave records can be searched on this site. Search can be conducted by name, location, or cemetery name.

Find a Grave: http://www.findagrave.com/

Interment.net - A free online database containing approximately 4 million cemetery records from around the world.

Interment.net: http://www.interment.net/

Billion Graves – as the name implies, you can search a billion records including headstone photos, transcriptions, cemetery records, and grave locations.

Billion Graves:
http://billiongraves.com/pages/search/index.php#cemetery

<u>Michigan Obituaries</u>

Obituaries can reveal a wealth about our ancestor and other relatives. You can search our **Michigan Newspaper Obituaries Listings** from hundreds of Michigan newspapers online for free.

Michigan Newspaper Obituaries Listings:
http://obituarieshelp.org/michigan_newspaper_obituaries.html

Michigan Wills and Probate Records

The documents found in a probate packet may include a complete inventory of a person's estate, newspaper entries, witness testimony, a copy of a will, list of debtors and creditors, names of executors or trustees, names of heirs. They can not only tell you about the ancestor you're currently researching, but lead to other ancestors.

Probate and matters of estate in Michigan were recorded by the clerk of the **Michigan Probate Courts** in each county.

Michigan Probate Courts:
http://www.wcpc.us/links/michiganprobatecourts_address.htm

Some county probate records dating from the early 19th century can be found at the **Archives of Michigan.**

Archives of Michigan:
http://www.michigan.gov/documents/mhc_sa_circular06_49689_7.p df

Family Search has the following index that can be searched online for free:

Michigan, Probate Records, 1797-1973:
https://familysearch.org/search/collection/2013878

Michigan Immigration and Naturalization Records

The naturalization process generated many types of records, including petitions, declarations of intention, and oaths of allegiance. These records can provide family historians with information such as a person's birth date and place of birth, immigration year, marital status, spouse information, occupation, witnesses' names and addresses, and more.

Archives of Michigan – county naturalizations and declarations of intent dating from mid-nineteenth century

Michigan Historical Center
702 West Kalamazoo St.
Lansing Michigan 48913
Tel: 517-373-3559
E-Mail: archives@michigan.gov
Archives of Michigan:
http://www.michigan.gov/documents/mhc_sa_circular10_49699_7.pdf

National Archives - Card Manifests of Entries through the Port of Detroit, MI, 1906-1954, Passenger and Alien Crew Lists of Vessels Arriving at the Port of Detroit, MI, 1946—1957

8601 Adelphi Road
College Park, MD 20740-6001
Tel: 1-866-272-6272

National Archives:
http://www.archives.gov/research/immigration/immigration-records-1891-1957.html

Family Search has the following index that can be searched online for free:

Michigan, Detroit Manifests of Arrivals at the Port of Detroit, 1906-1954: https://familysearch.org/search/collection/1916040

Michigan Native American Records

Archives of Michigan – wide variety of records, studies, and other data related to tge Native American tribes of Michigan

702 West Kalamazoo St.
P.O. Box 30740, Lansing, MI 48909
517-373-1408
archives@michigan.gov

Archives of Michigan:
http://www.michigan.gov/documents/mhc_sa_circular30_50002_7.pdf

Access Genealogy – Michigan Native American census records, tribal histories, and much more:
http://www.accessgenealogy.com/native/michigan-indian-tribes.htm

U.S. National Archives - information on American Indians who maintained their ties to Federally-recognized Tribes (1830-1970).

U.S. National Archives: http://www.archives.gov/research/native-americans/

Records of the Bureau of Indian Affairs (BIA):
http://www.archives.gov/research/guide-fed-records/groups/075.html

American Indians Records Repository - records dating from the 1700s including trust, education and other historic Indian Affairs records
American Indian Records Repository
Meritex Enterprises
17501 West 98th Street
Lenexa, KS 66219
Phone: 913-888-0601

American Indians Records Repository:
http://www.doi.gov/ost/records_mgmt/american-indian-records-repository.cfm

Missing Matriarchs – Resources for Researching Female Michigan Ancestors

Looking for female ancestors requires an adjustment of how we view traditional records sources. A woman's identity was often under that of her husband, and often individual records for them can be difficult to locate. The following resources are effective in locating female ancestors in Michigan where traditional records may not reveal them.

<u>Bibliographies</u>

- *In Detroit…Courage Was the Fashion: The Contributing Women to the Development of Detroit from 1701 to 1951,* Alice T. Coratheru (Wayne State University Press, 1953)
- *Black Women in the Middle West: The Michigan Experience,* Darlene Clark Hine (Indiana Historical Bureau, 1986)
- *Birchbark Belles: Women on the Michigan Frontier,* Larry B. Massie (Priscilla Press, 1993)
- *True Sisterhood: Michigan Women and Their Kin, 1820-1920,* Marilyn Ferris, Motz (State University of New York Press, 1983)

Selected Resources for Michigan Women's History

Michigan Historical Center
702 West Kalamazoo St.
Lansing Michigan 48913

Eli Sharp Museum
3225 Fourth St.
Jackson, MI 49203

Michigan Women's History Center
213 Main St.
Lansing, MI 48933

Common Michigan Surnames

The following surnames are among the most common in Michigan and are also being currently researched by other genealogists. If you find your surname here, there is a chance that some research has already been performed on your ancestor.

Alcona, Alger, Allegan, Alpena, Antrim, Arenac, Baraga, Barry, Bay, Benzie, Berrien, Branch, Calhoun, Cass, Charlevoix, Cheboygan, Chippewa, Clare, Clinton, Crawford, Delta, Dickinson, Eaton, Emmet, Genesee, Gladwin, Gogebic, Grand, Gratiot, Hillsdale, Houghton, Huron, Ingham, Ionia, Iosco, Iron, Isabella, Jackson, Kalamazoo, Kalkaska, Kent, Keweenaw, Lake, Lapeer, Leelanau, Lenawee, Livingston, Luce, Mackinac, Macomb, Manistee, Marquette, Mason, Mecosta, Menominee, Midland, Missaukee, Monroe, Montcalm, Montmorency, Muskegon, Newaygo, Oakland, Oceana, Ogemaw, Ontonagon, Osceola, Oscoda, Otsego, Ottawa, Presque, Roscommon, Saginaw, Sanilac, ,Schoolcraft, Shiawassee, St. Clair, St. Joseph, Tuscola, VanBuren, Washtenaw, Wayne, Wexford

Notes

Notes